What on Earth? Lightning

What on Earth?

Thunder crack crash!

Lightning!

You are inside your house during a thunderstorm. What should—and shouldn't—you do?

Turn the page and find out!

Published in 2005 in the United States by Children's Press,
an imprint of Scholastic Library Publishing,
90 Sherman Turnpike, Danbury, CT 06816

ISBN 0-516-25322-0 (Lib. Bdg)

A CIP catalogue record for this title is available now from the Library of Congress.

Printed and bound in China.

Editors:	Ronald Coleman
	Sophie Izod
Senior Art Editor:	Carolyn Franklin
DTP Designer:	Mark Williams

Picture Credits Dave Antram: 23(b), Julian Baker & Janet
Baker (J B Illustrations): 7, 8, 9, Mark Bergin: 12, 13, 21,
24, Elizabeth Branch: 10, 14, 22, 16-17, Hans Wiborg
Jenssen: 25, Craig Aurness/Corbis: 26, Dan Griggs/NHPA:
6, Art Archive/Chateau De Blerancourt/Dagli Orti: 25,
Corbis: 8-9, 11, 15, 18, 23, 27, 30-31, Digital Vision: 19, 28,
29, PhotoDisc: 18

Cover © Craig Aurness/Corbis

What on Earth?

Lightning?

Turn off your computer
and stay away from open
doors and windows. Do
not talk on the phone or
run water.

What on Earth? Lightning

Brian Williams

How often does lightning hit Earth?

Turn to page 15 and find out!

children's press®

A Division of Scholastic Inc.

NEW YORK • TORONTO • LONDON • AUCKLAND • SYDNEY
MEXICO CITY • NEW DELHI • HONG KONG
DANBURY, CONNECTICUT

Contents

What on Earth?

How much energy is in a thunderstorm?

A typical thunderstorm has more energy than ten small nuclear bombs!

Shocking energy!

Introduction

A bolt of lightning in a dark stormy sky is one of the most amazing sights in nature. A lightning bolt is a gigantic **electrical spark** that leaps from a thundercloud and crackles across the sky. It is the most visible form of electricity. Lightning occurs when some of the electrical energy inside a thundercloud **bursts** free in a blinding flash of light.

Are clouds electric?

No, clouds are made of rain, hail or snow. Fierce winds blow inside a storm cloud causing water droplets and ice crystals to **crash** together violently. This creates static electricity which builds up inside the cloud.

Is electricity everywhere?

Yes. Everything in the universe is made of atoms which contain tiny charged particles that can create **tingles** of static electricity. You can see this if you rub a balloon on your hair and put it against a wall. An electrical force holds the balloon to the wall!

What Makes Lightning?

Inside a thundercloud there are two kinds of **electrical energy**. Positive (+) electrical charges are lighter, so they rise to the top of the cloud, and negative (-) electrical charges are heavier, so they sink to the bottom. When a positive (+) charge and a negative (-) charge "jump" together we see lightning.

How much power?

A flash of lightning can contain about 1 billion volts of electricity. Your TV uses 120 volts.

Positively charged

Positive (+) electrical charges whirl around near the top of a thundercloud, where it is coldest.

Thundercloud

Negatively charged

Negative (-) electrical charges build up near the bottom of the cloud.

Positively electrical!

An electical impulse called a "leader" comes down from the cloud and attracts a positive charge from the ground called a "streamer" which jumps up to meet it.

Positively charged Earth

Where Does Lightning Strike?

Thunder and lightning occur during storms. Storms are caused by hot air rising and cold air rushing in to fill the space. As the ice at the top of a cloud is tossed around it creates an electrical charge and you get lightning. Most areas on Earth have storms.

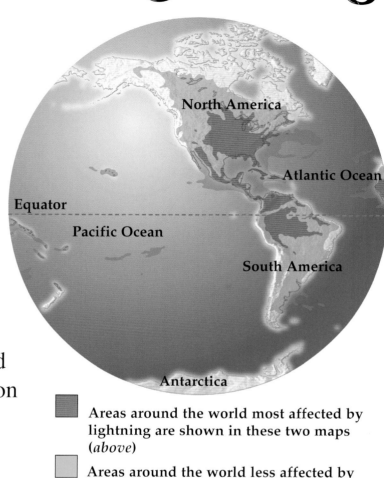

North America

Atlantic Ocean

Equator

Pacific Ocean

South America

Antarctica

Areas around the world most affected by lightning are shown in these two maps (*above*)

Areas around the world less affected by lightning are shown in the maps

Baked Alaska?

In June 2004, a record-breaking 17,000 lightning strikes hit Alaska, starting hundreds of fires.

Where are the most thunderstorms?

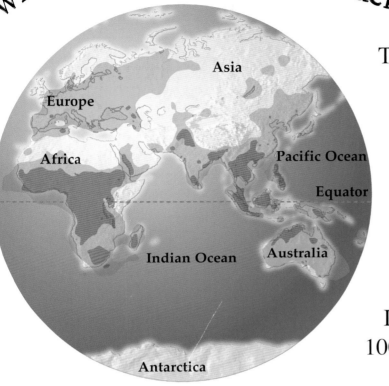

- Asia
- Europe
- Africa
- Pacific Ocean
- Equator
- Indian Ocean
- Australia
- Antarctica

Thunderstorms are most common near the equator. This is because it's hotter there, so there is more hot air rising and creating more thunderclouds and lightning. Areas closest to the equator such as South America, Central Africa and Indonesia have an average of 100-200 thunderstorms a year.

Lightning in space?

Flashes of lightning have been seen on Venus and Jupiter. Lightning on Jupiter is thought to be more powerful than on Earth but happens less often.

Is Lightning Dangerous?

Lightning is electricity. An electric shock can kill you, and the electricity in lightning is very strong. In the United States, about 1,000 people a year are injured by lightning, and around 100 people are killed each year. People who are struck by lightning can die from heart attacks or from being burned.

What should you do in a thunderstorm?

Try to get inside. If you can't, stay away from trees. Also, never hold metal objects like umbrellas because metal objects attract lightning.

Why shouldn't you seek shelter under a tree?

During a thunderstorm never shelter under a lone tree or on top of a hill. Lightning usually strikes the highest point as it seeks the shortest path to earth.

Hotter than the sun?

Lightning heats the air around it to about 54,000° F. This is hotter than the Sun!

Lightning, sign of the Gods?

Lightning is awesome, so it's not surprising that many years ago people believed it was created by the gods. The ancient Greeks thought lightning was a sign of the gods' anger. They thought places hit by lightning were sacred and built temples there. The Vikings of northern Europe believed the god Thor caused thunder and lightning by throwing his hammer.

Why did Zeus have thunderbolts?

The Greeks believed that Zeus, king of the gods, showed his anger by hurling thunderbolts down to Earth to remind humans that he was all-powerful.

Protection from the god of thunder!

Vikings wore lucky charms for protection. The wearer believed that Thor would not hurl lightning at them!

Yule log!

People thought wood from a "lightning-blasted" tree would protect them. In Europe, the Christmas "Yule log" is burned for luck, as well as protection from lightning.

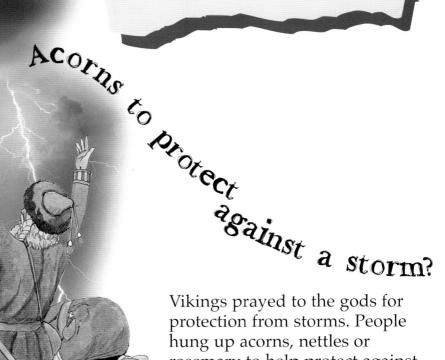

Acorns to protect against a storm?

Vikings prayed to the gods for protection from storms. People hung up acorns, nettles or rosemary to help protect against thunder and lightning.

Is Lightning Always Forked?

Forked or zig-zag are the most common forms, but there are many different kinds of lightning. Sheet lightning is a flash from one thundercloud to another. Ball lightning is a small ball of light which can fly or hover inside buildings and planes! Some aircraft pilots have seen "sprites" or "rocket lightning" – long streaks of lightning that shoot up in the sky from a cloud, but these are very rare.

How many types of lightning are there?

Forked lightning looks like the letter Y upside down.

Zig-zag lightning is a giant spark that zig-zags its way to the ground.

Sheet lightning makes a white light that fills a wide area of the sky.

Ball lightning is a slow moving ball of fire that can sometimes appear inside buildings and planes.

St. Elmo's Fire is a faint flickering glow around trees, buildings or ships' masts.

What on Earth?

News flash

A flash of lightning hits Earth about 100 times every second, but only about one out of every four bolts hits the ground. Most lightning leaps from one cloud to another.

What Is Thunder?

Thunder is one of the loudest sounds in nature. It is made when the hot air inside a thundercloud expands and vibrates. This makes the loud rumbling crash that we call thunder. Thunder and lightning happen at the same time but you see the flash of light before you hear the crash of thunder. This is because light travels many times faster than sound.

Flash-to-BANG!

Count the seconds from the flash of lightning to the bang of thunder. Divide this by 5 for miles (by 3 for kilometers) and you'll know how many miles (or kilometers) away the storm is.

Raining cats and dogs?

No, fish and frogs!

People have stories of all sorts of weird objects falling from thunderclouds, including live fish and tiny frogs! These small animals can be sucked up from ponds by whirling winds into a storm cloud – and then fall back down with the rain.

Does Lightning Strike Twice?

It is said that "lightning **never strikes** twice", but in fact it can hit the same place many times. Tall skyscrapers are hit by lightning many times each year.

Unlucky **elephants**!

Elephants aren't always lucky. In 1999, seven elephants in Kruger National Park, South Africa, were killed by the same lightning strike.

What on Earth?

Seven times unlucky!

An unlucky park ranger named Roy Sullivan has been struck by lightning seven times! His injuries include burnt eyebrows, scorched hair and stomach burns. He's lucky to be alive!

Can Planes Fly Through Lightning?

Small planes can be damaged inside a storm cloud. Fortunately, larger aircraft flying through electrical storms are rarely hit by lightning. If lightning does strike, it usually spreads harmlessly over the plane's metal body. However, in 1963 over Maryland, a jet airliner was struck killing 82 people on board. It is the highest **death toll** caused by a single lightning strike.

Could a plane be smashed in a thundercloud?

Yes, howling winds inside a thundercloud whirl around so fast, they could break up a small plane.

Blob lightning!

In 1984, Russian airline passengers were surprised to see a blob of ball lightning floating over their heads inside the plane! No one was hurt but the plane's radar was affected.

What on Earth?

Your flight is delayed!

In 1969, the *Apollo 12* spacecraft was hit by lightning as it took off for the Moon. It survived. But in 1987, a rocket launched from Florida crashed after lightning damaged its on-board computer. Space shuttle launches are now postponed when lightning is expected.

Lightning rod

Is Lightning Useful?

Scientists cannot yet catch lightning to hold the electricity. But lightning does enrich the Earth's soil. A lightning flash causes nitrogen and oxygen in the air to bind together. The **nitrogen-rich** raindrops that fall to the ground help fertilize the soil. All plants and animals need nitrogen, and in this way lightning may have helped to create life on Earth.

Fire from the sky!

Prehistoric people probably first discovered fire after lightning struck and set fire to tree branches during a storm.

shock horror!

In Mary Shelley's book *Frankenstein*, Dr. Frankenstein uses lightning to bring his monster to life!

What Is a Lightning Rod?

High buildings and public places are often protected by lightning rods. A metal spike is fixed to the highest point of a building. A copper or aluminum strip runs down from the top to wires buried in the ground below. If lightning strikes, it travels down the rod into the ground, leaving the building unharmed.

Do tall towers get struck?

Lightning usually strikes the highest point, so tall buildings are an easy target. The Empire State Building in New York is hit by lightning about 100 times each year. But it is protected by a lightning rod, so there's no damage. Because the lightning rod provides a safe path for lightning to flow, it even protects smaller buildings nearby.

CN Tower Toronto, Canada

Sears Tower Chicago, USA

Eiffel Tower Paris, France

Empire State Building New York, USA

Petronas Towers Kuala Lumpur, Malaysia

What on Earth?

Melting rocks!

Lightning generates enormous heat. When a bolt of lightning hits the ground, it is so hot that it can melt solid rock!

Who invented the lightning rod?

Benjamin Franklin (*below*) proved that lightning was electricity. He invented the lightning rod in 1752. The first lightning rod was put on a house in the same year.

The new idea travels!

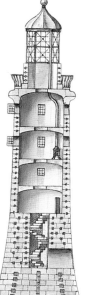

Eddystone Rock Lighthouse near Plymouth, England, was built in 1759 to replace an old wooden lighthouse destroyed by lightning. In 1750 it was the first building in England to have a lightning rod.

How Fast Does Lightning Travel?

When lightning flashes, it finds the fastest path down to Earth and then it follows the same route back up to the cloud again. A downward flash of lightning (the leader) travels at up to 994 miles (1,600 kilometers) per second. The return or upward speed is even faster at up to 86,990 miles (140,000 kilometers) per second!

Thunder travels much more slowly. A thunderclap moves at the speed of sound, about 1,148 feet (350 meters) per second.

How Would You Survive In a Lightning Storm?

Some people have been struck by a small flash of lightning and not even noticed it, while others were thrown into the air and had their clothes burned. Follow these rules to avoid being hit by lightning.

What to do Checklist

Make sure you are inside a **building** as the walls will channel the lightning to the Earth. Use a **radio** to keep track of storms. Use the **Flash-to-Bang** method (see page 17) to find out how close you are to the lightning. If you can't get inside, make yourself a small target, crouch down with only your feet touching the ground and cover your head.

Lightning dangers

Telephones Lightning can pass through the wiring and can kill the person speaking.

Open spaces Lightning tries to find the quickest route to earth, if you are the tallest thing around it may use you! Find shelter immediately.

Swimming Water conducts electricity, which means swimming is very dangerous during storms. Leave the water as soon as possible.

Lightning Facts

In 1977, an aircraft flew into a thunderstorm and all four engines stopped. Lightning struck and the propellers started turning again.

People fishing are more likely to be hit by lightning than golfers. Both are at risk because they are holding metal, and out in the open.

A bolt of lightning is only about 1 inch (2.5 cm) wide.

At any one moment, 2,000 thunderstorms are likely to be happening around the Earth.

There's an area of Florida that is struck by lightning so often, people call it Lightning Alley.

Saguaro cacti are very tall and are often struck by lightning. The water inside the cactus boils in a split-second, and the cactus explodes!

If there's less than 30 seconds between the flash and the bang, seek shelter. Stay inside for 30 minutes after the last thunderclap. This is called the 30/30 rule.

Glossary

aluminum metal that conducts electricity

atom smallest part of an element (matter), made up of a nucleus, protons and electrons

copper a metal that conducts electricity easily

electricity energy in the form of moving electrons

equator imaginary line around Earth's widest part

insulation material that blocks the passage of heat or electricity

leader the part of lightning that comes down out of a cloud

lightning rod a metal spike that attracts electricity

nitrogen colorless gas that makes up 80% of the atmosphere (our air)

particle very tiny piece of matter, smaller than an atom

static electricity charge of electricity that does not flow as a current along a wire

streamer the part of lightning that shoots up from an object on the ground

superstitions beliefs based on folklore and myth

volt a measurement of electrical power

watt a measurement of electrical power

What Do You Know About Lightning?

1. What makes thunder?

2. Should you shelter under a tree during a thunderstorm?

3. Who was the Norse god of thunder and lightning?

4. Where are thunderstorms most common?

5. Which lightning is most common?

6. Which travels fastest, thunder or lightning?

7. Who survived the most lightning strikes?

8. Can lightning affect space rockets?

9. Whose monster was brought to life by lightning?

10. Who made the first lightning rod?

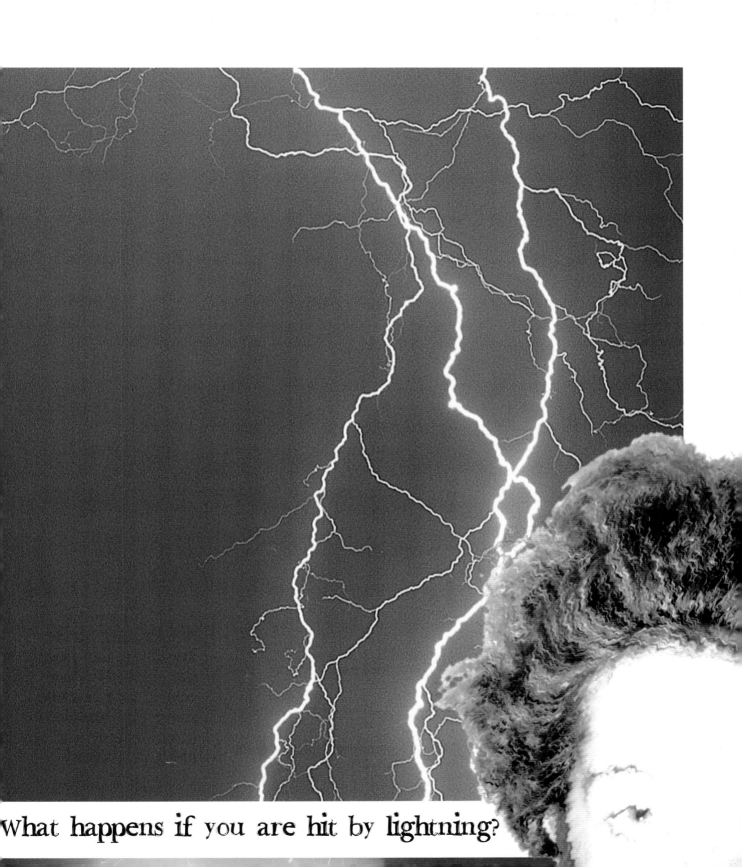

What happens if you are hit by lightning?

Index

Pictures are shown in **bold**.

Answers

1. Hot vibrating air in a cloud (See page 16)
2. No. Lightning is attracted to tall objects (See page 10)
3. Thor (See page 12)
4. Near the equator (See page 9)
5. Forked or zig-zag lightning (See page 14)
6. Lightning (See page 16)
7. American park ranger Roy Sullivan – seven times! (See page 19)
8. Yes, it can crash their computers (See page 21)
9. Dr. Frankenstein's (See page 23)
10. Benjamin Franklin (See page 25)

A lightning strike knocks many people to the ground. Some people are burned, some are knocked unconscious, and some are even killed.